VOL 2

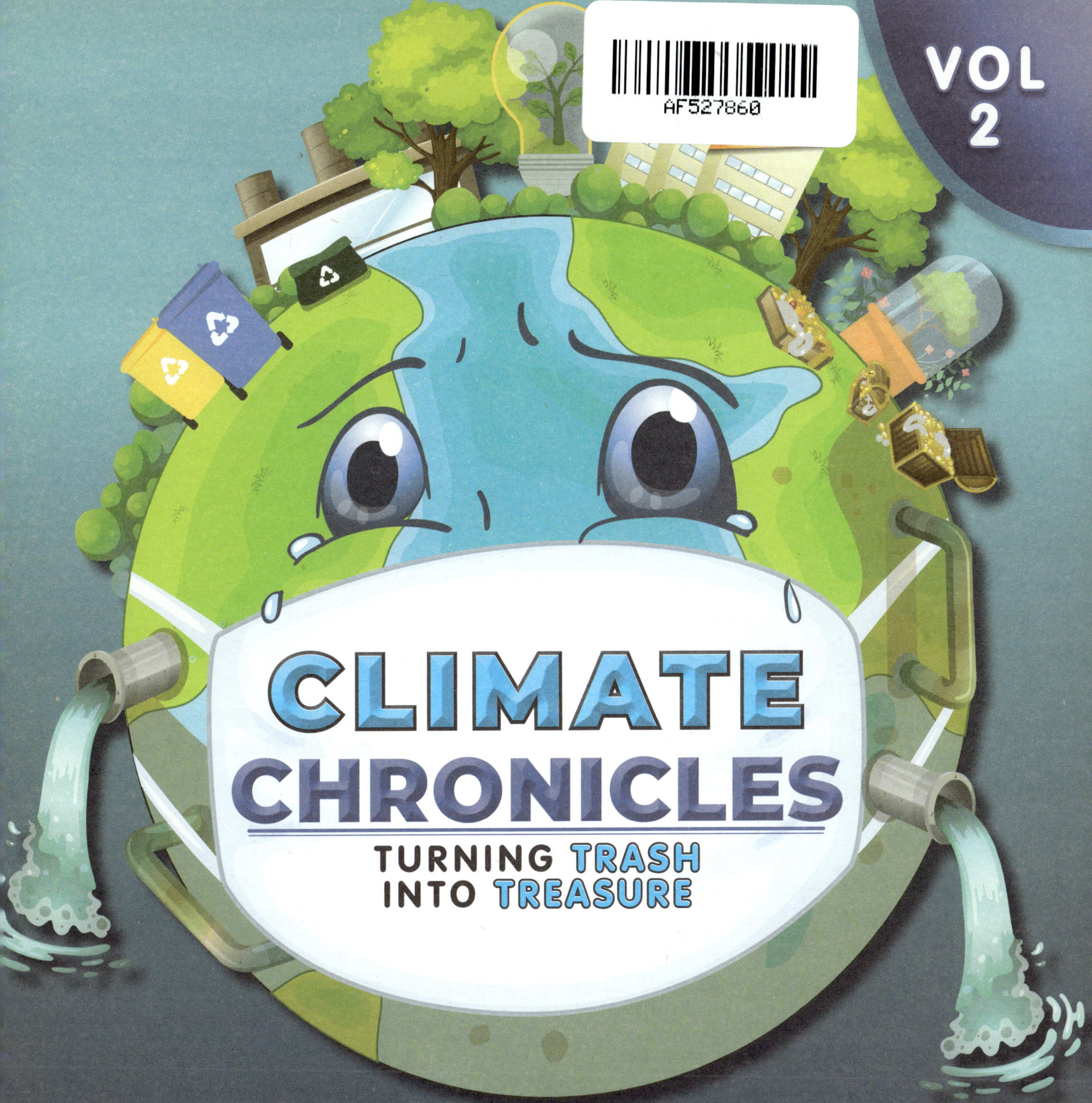

CLIMATE CHRONICLES

TURNING TRASH INTO TREASURE

MOONSTONE

Published in Moonstone
by Rupa Publications India Pvt. Ltd 2024
7/16, Ansari Road, Daryaganj
New Delhi 110002

Sales centres:
Bengaluru Chennai
Hyderabad Jaipur Kathmandu
Kolkata Mumbai Prayagraj

P-ISBN: 978-93-6156-697-4
E-ISBN: 978-93-6156-378-2

First impression 2024

10 9 8 7 6 5 4 3 2 1

Printed in India

Contents

Contents

RENEWABLE ENERGY

Introduction

Global warming leads to drastic weather shifts, like glacier melting, droughts, heatwaves, erratic rainfall, and seasonal alterations. The layer of greenhouse gases (GHGs) surrounding the Earth thickens daily, trapping excess heat. Burning fossil fuels for energy is the primary GHG emitter. Continuing this trend could escalate global warming to a critical level. Additionally, fossil fuels, being non-renewable, will eventually deplete.

Hence, conserving fossil fuels is imperative. To do so, we must seek renewable energy alternatives. These sources, such as solar, wind, hydro, and geothermal power, are naturally replenished and hold immense energy potential. Unlike fossil fuels, they emit no harmful pollutants, making them environmentally friendly.

Fossil Fuels

Fossil fuels, formed from ancient plant and animal remains, originated in Earth's past swamps and bogs. As these organisms died, they were buried under layers of mud, sand, and silt. Over time, decomposition turned them into organic materials, ultimately creating fossil fuels.

Main Fossil Fuels

Coal, oil, and natural gas are the primary fossil fuels. Coal, a readily combustible rock, exists in underground layers known as coal beds. Crude oil, often foul-smelling and yellow or black, typically resides in underground reservoirs. Natural gas, predominantly composed of methane, is a blend of various gases.

Source of World's energy

Over 90% of our energy needs are fulfilled by fossil fuels. They are primarily utilised to generate electricity, a vital component of daily life. Additionally, they power vehicles, provide heating for homes, and drive industrial processes.

Contributor to Warming

Burning coal, oil, and natural gas releases billions of tonnes of carbon dioxide and other harmful greenhouse gases into the atmosphere, leading to ozone layer depletion and global warming.

FUN FACT

Coal accounts for nearly half of all the resources used in the generation of electricity.

? Coal occurs in layers below the earth called __________.

Petroleum and Natural Gas Formation

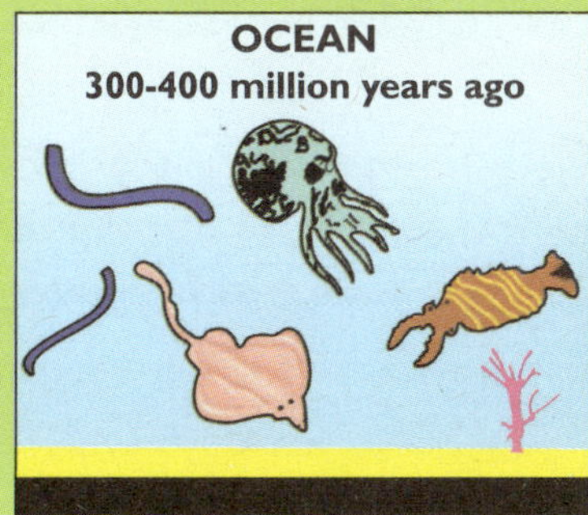

Tiny sea plants and animals died and were buried in the ocean floor. Over time, they were covered by layers of silt and sand.

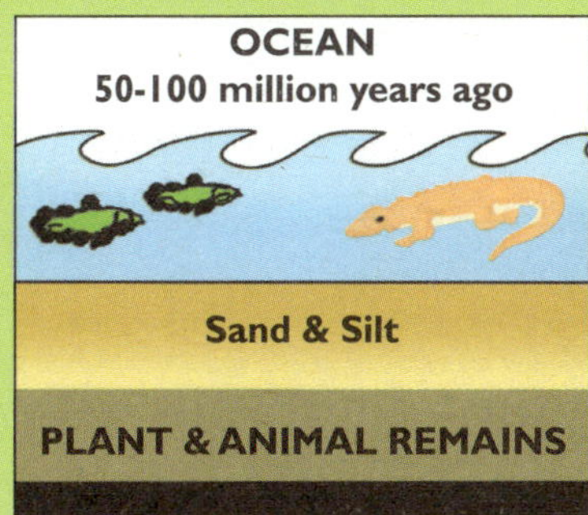

Over millions of years, the remains were buried deeper and deeper. The enormous heat and pressure turned them into oil and gas.

Today, we drill down through layers of sand, silt and rock to reach the rock formation that contains oil and gas deposits.

Future Energy Needs

Currently, around 80-85% of the world's energy comes from fossil fuels, while renewable sources contribute just 15-20%. As energy demand grows, the reliance on fossil fuels is expected to increase, worsening global warming due to the large CO2 emissions they produce.

Future Energy Needs

By 2040, industrial energy consumption is projected to surge by 28%, while residential and commercial energy needs are expected to rise by approximately 30%. Transportation demands across industries are anticipated to increase by around 45%. Given this rapid escalation in energy demands, urgent efforts are required to develop alternative energy sources.

Future Projections

According to the Intergovernmental Panel on Climate Change (IPCC), established by the World Meteorological Organization (WMO), continued high rates of fossil fuel consumption could raise global temperatures by 3.4 to 6.1°C during the 21st century. Sea levels may rise by 18 to 59 centimetres, leading to more frequent hurricanes, storms, floods, and droughts. The melting ice caps would also reduce freshwater availability, exacerbating shortages. Habitat loss could drive many plant and animal species to extinction.

FUN FACT

Through the first half of the twentieth century, global warming was thought to be good for countries with very low temperatures.

? ______________ of world's energy comes from fossil fuels.

Solar Energy

Throughout history, humans have utilised solar energy in various ways. However, with the discovery of fossil fuels, there was a shift away from solar energy. In recent decades, as the limitations and negative impacts of fossil fuels have become apparent, there has been a renewed interest in harnessing solar power.

Solar Thermal Power Plants

Solar power plants harness electricity from solar energy using mirrors and lenses to concentrate sunlight into a high-intensity beam, resulting in elevated temperatures. This heat is utilised to boil water, powering a steam turbine that generates electricity without emitting harmful pollutants.

Solar Solution

Solar energy, a sustainable alternative to fossil fuels, can generate electricity without combustion. It can also replace fossil fuels in cooking, water heating, and space heating.

Photovoltaic cells

Solar panels, constructed from photovoltaic cells (PV), are a widely used technology for transforming solar energy into electricity. Comprised of semiconductor materials like silicon, these cells release electrons from their atoms when exposed to sunlight, generating electricity through the flow of electrons.

FUN FACT

The Bhadla Solar Park, situated in the Jodhpur district of Rajasthan, is the world's largest solar plant, covering an expansive area of 14,000 acres.

? Name the world's largest solar plant.

____

Solar-powered Objects

Utilising less than 0.02% of available solar energy could suffice to substitute fossil fuels and nuclear power as energy sources. While smaller solar devices like solar cookers and calculators are already in use, larger technologies such as solar cars remain a vision for the future.

Solar Cookers

Solar cookers utilise direct sunlight or heat to cook food, offering a cost-effective and fuel-efficient alternative. The increasing awareness of fossil fuel conservation has contributed to the growing popularity of these low-tech devices.

Solar Cars

Solar cars, still in development, resemble long, wide, and flat tabletops on wheels. Automobile emissions rank second globally as a cause of global warming. Solar cars, powered by electricity generated from their solar panels, offer a promising solution by eliminating CO_2 emissions associated with conventional vehicles.

? Solar lamps can also be used to charge ________.

Solar Lamps

Solar lamps, connected to solar panels, provide light and can charge mobile phones, particularly beneficial for those without access to electricity. Solar cells power these lamps.

FUN FACT

The Vanguard 1 satellite, launched in 1958, was the first spacecraft to use solar panels.

Passive Solar Energy

Passive solar energy, which harnesses sunlight directly for heating and lighting buildings, doesn't require mechanical or electrical devices. The design of a building is pivotal in maximising its utilisation of solar energy.

Passive Solar Heating

Buildings can be strategically designed to capture and retain solar heat through well-placed windows, heat-absorbing materials in floors and walls, and effective insulation. With such design considerations, a building can potentially meet nearly all its heating requirements using solar energy, as suggested by the New Mexico Solar Energy Association.

Passive Solar Building Design

Traditional homes often lack efficient design features to harness natural light effectively. By constructing energy-efficient houses that naturally capture solar energy for heating in winter and cooling in summer, we can combat global warming. These homes reduce reliance on fossil fuels by reducing the need for electricity-powered heating and cooling systems.

Passive Cooling

Strategies such as minimising window size and incorporating reflective materials in external walls and roofs are employed for passive cooling of any building. Shading elements such as eaves or vegetation help deflect solar radiation, further enhancing cooling efficiency.

FUN FACT

External shading devices have the potential to decrease a building's heat gains by up to 90%.

? Solar energy can be used for heating a house without any device. (True/False)

Solar Heating in Homes

While our homes don't emit pollutants, they still add to global warming. The electricity we use comes from power plants burning fossil fuels. We can help combat global warming by reducing fossil fuel use and using devices like solar water heaters and ovens.

Solar Pool Heaters

A solar pool heater can warm water in a swimming pool by circulating it through solar panels, where it absorbs heat from the sun before being returned to the pool. This system can reduce greenhouse gas emissions by 5-10 tonnes per year.

Solar Water Heaters

Currently, solar water heating systems provide hot water for over 70 million households worldwide. In regions with very cold climates, where significant energy is used to heat household water, solar water heaters offer a substantial reduction in reliance on fossil fuels.

FUN FACT

A solar oven can be homemade by enclosing a cardboard box with layers of insulation and aluminum foil wrapping.

Solar Space Heating Systems

Space heating warms a building's interior using solar collectors on rooftops that gather and distribute solar thermal energy through solid or liquid bases via pumps, fans, and blowers.

? Space heating warms a building's ___________ using solar collectors.

Solar Energy in Space

The sun provides a vast and dependable source of energy. With growing awareness of global warming, there's a concerted effort to harness solar energy for our daily requirements. Researchers worldwide are exploring methods to capture solar energy in space and utilise it here on Earth.

Transportation

In regions like the Sahara Desert, abundant solar energy is available but faces challenges in transportation to high-demand areas. Space-based solar power aims to address this by targeting hard-to-reach regions. Scientists propose using microwaves or lasers to transmit collected energy from space to specific Earth locations, minimising the need for ground-based energy storage.

Advantages

Solar power plants on Earth can collect solar power for only 6-8 hours a day, whereas in a space-based power plant, solar power can be collected throughout the day. Additionally, energy collection in space is not influenced by changes in weather or time of day, as it is on Earth.

? The energy collected in space can be beamed back to earth through microwaves and __________.

FUN FACT

Dezhou can be referred to as a "solar city" because the majority of its population utilises solar hot water systems and solar electricity.

Wind Energy

The utilisation of wind energy for power generation is not a recent development. Humans recognised its significant potential as an energy source centuries ago. Nonetheless, there is a continued need to discover additional methods to harness wind energy efficiently to combat global warming.

Wind Power for Electricity

Wind power currently supplies around 3.7% of the world's electricity, growing at an annual rate of almost 36%. By 2012, 100 countries were using wind energy for electricity production. Denmark relies on wind for nearly 42.1% of its electricity, Portugal for 24%, Spain for 20.2%, Ireland for 21.1%, and Germany for 13.3%. This has reduced their fossil fuel consumption, consequently lowering greenhouse gas emissions.

Wind Turbines

Windmills evolved into what we now call wind turbines, which can reach heights equivalent to a twenty-storey building and feature long blades. Wind turbines harness the force of winds to spin their blades, converting this motion energy into electricity through a generator.

Early Uses

Our ancestors utilized wind energy for tasks like grinding grain and pumping underground water. Between the 18th and 19th centuries, humans realised wind power could generate electricity. The first electricity-producing windmill was constructed in Scotland in July 1887 by Professor James Blyth, who used it to light his cottage.

FUN FACT

Nearly one-fifth of Denmark's electricity is generated by wind turbines.

? ________________ built the first windmill for producing electricity.

Wind Farms

Wind farms are locations where tens or sometimes hundreds of wind turbines are grouped together to generate electricity. They are beneficial for the environment as they produce electricity in a clean and non-polluting manner.

The Hurdle of Location

Coastal areas, hilltops, and open plains offer the best locations for wind farms due to their stronger and more consistent winds. The main challenge in harnessing wind energy is its irregularity.

Offshore Wind Farms

Some turbines are constructed on water bodies, mounted to the seabed through long towers. They are more efficient than land-based turbines in harnessing wind power because winds blow at higher speeds over water bodies. Offshore wind turbine technology has rapidly advanced in recent years.

Floating Wind Turbines

Floating farms, developed in the mid-1990s, offer a solution to the limitations of traditional offshore wind farms. They can float in waters as deep as 700 metres (almost 2,300 feet), taking advantage of strong winds in the middle of the ocean.

FUN FACT

The Gansu Wind Farm in China is the largest wind farm in the world, with a target capacity of 20,000 MW.

? Some wind turbines can harness wind energy while floating in water. (True/False)

Geothermal Energy

Geothermal energy is heat stored within the Earth, with some regions having higher concentrations. The most active resources are found where underground temperatures are highest, sometimes emerging as volcanoes and hot springs.

Geothermal Power Plants

Dry steam plants, flash steam plants, and binary cycle power plants are the three types of geothermal power plants. They extract dry steam or hot water from deep below the Earth's surface through wells and pipes. This steam or water is used to turn generator turbines and produce electricity.

Geothermal Heat Pumps

A common use of geothermal energy is heating or cooling buildings with geothermal heat pumps, also known as ground source heat pumps (GSHP). These pumps transfer heat from the ground or water into buildings during winters, and in summers, the process is reversed.

FUN FACT

The first geothermal power plant was built in 1904 in Larderello, Tuscany, Italy.

? Where was the first geothermal plant built? ________________

Geothermal Energy in Future

Many governments are promoting geothermal energy as a future alternative. The US government provides financial aid to organisations opting for geothermal resources instead of fossil fuels. Those still reliant on fossil fuels incur higher costs.

Economic Boost

In the US, the world leader in geothermal electricity production, approximately 3,591 megawatts of energy per year are generated from geothermal sources, resulting in $1 billion in revenue. Indonesia, with significant potential, aims to produce 29,215 megawatts of geothermal energy annually, contributing $7.3 billion in revenue each year.

Iceland: A Unique Example

Iceland's abundance of volcanoes makes it rich in geothermal energy. Approximately 90% of homes in Iceland are heated using geothermal energy. Six geothermal power plants in the country produce around 27% of its electricity, with the remainder primarily coming from hydropower.

?

Name the country that produces the maximum geothermal energy.

____

A Future Alternative?

The cost of geothermal energy production is decreasing, making it a viable option for the future. Some facilities have cut electricity prices by 50% since 1980. The direct use of geothermal resources for heating and cooling homes holds promise, and ongoing technological advancements in harnessing geothermal energy will enhance its utility as a future alternative.

FUN FACT

Ninety percent of the world's geothermal plants are located along the "Ring of Fire," a horseshoe-shaped zone encircling the Pacific Ocean.

Marine Energy-I

Marine energy, or ocean energy, holds significant potential for powering homes and industries through the kinetic energy generated by ocean water movement. The four primary sources of marine energy are tidal energy, wave energy, ocean thermal energy, and osmotic energy.

Power of Oceans

Scientists suggest that ocean energy has the potential to provide ten million terawatt-hours of electricity annually. Once fully developed, the clean and non-polluting energy from oceans could significantly mitigate global warming.

FUN FACT

The Sihwa Lake Tidal Power Station in South Korea is the world's largest tidal power plant.

? Name the largest tidal power plant of the world? ____________

Tidal Power

Tidal energy has been utilized since the 11th century. The significant increase in water level between low and high tides can be used to generate energy. There are two methods to harness tidal energy: utilising dams or barrages to exploit the rise and fall of sea levels, and using marine turbines to capture the energy of tidal currents.

Ocean Thermal Energy

The sun's warmth heats the ocean's surface water more than the deep water, creating thermal energy that can power heat engines for electricity. Many countries are testing and developing this technology, with ocean thermal energy having the potential to generate thousands of terawatt-hours of power annually.

Marine Energy-II

Currently, ocean energy usage is limited, with only a few small plants worldwide. However, it has garnered significant interest from scientists due to its vast potential in combating global warming. Efforts are underway to develop technologies for effectively harnessing marine energy.

Osmotic Power

The blending of freshwater and seawater where a river meets the ocean releases significant energy that can be harnessed for power production with minimal environmental impact. Osmotic energy is estimated to have the capacity to generate around 2000 terawatt-hours of electricity annually.

Wave Energy

In many parts of the world, strong winds generate continuous waves, with pressure fluctuations below the surface also playing a role. Ocean waves contain significant energy potential, estimated at 2-3 million megawatts globally, enough to supply 10 percent of the world's electricity. However, harnessing this energy is challenging due to the waves' high energy content.

Harnessing Wave energy

Both deep and shallow sea waters experience waves, making them potential sources of wave power. Devices designed to capture wave energy can be installed on shorelines, offshore, and far offshore locations. The shoreline device for capturing wave energy is called the oscillating water column (OWC). Aqua Buoy and Wave Dragon are two common devices that harness energy from deep-water waves.

FUN FACT

Poseidon in Denmark is a floating power plant that produces both wave energy and wind energy.

? ______________ is a shoreline device used for capturing wave energy.

Hydropower

Thousands of years ago, the ancient Greeks, Romans, Arabs, Chinese, and Indians used water wheels for grinding grains. Watermills, powered by waterwheels, were used to crush sugarcane to make sugar and to pound wood into pulp. During the nineteenth century, water turbines were developed to produce electricity.

Production of Hydroelectricity

The electricity generated using hydropower is called hydroelectricity. Huge concrete structures called dams are built on rivers to capture hydropower, blocking river flow and creating vast reservoirs. Water released from a reservoir flows through a turbine, spinning it, which then activates a generator to produce electricity. Small hydropower plants channel river water through a turbine using a canal.

Hydropower Combats Global Warming

Approximately one-fifth of the world's electricity comes from hydropower plants, reducing greenhouse gas emissions by around 20% compared to fossil fuels. China, Brazil, Canada, and the United States are the largest hydroelectric power producers. China's Three Gorges Dam, generating 22,500 megawatts, is the world's largest hydroelectric dam.

? _______________ is the largest hydroelectric dam in the world.

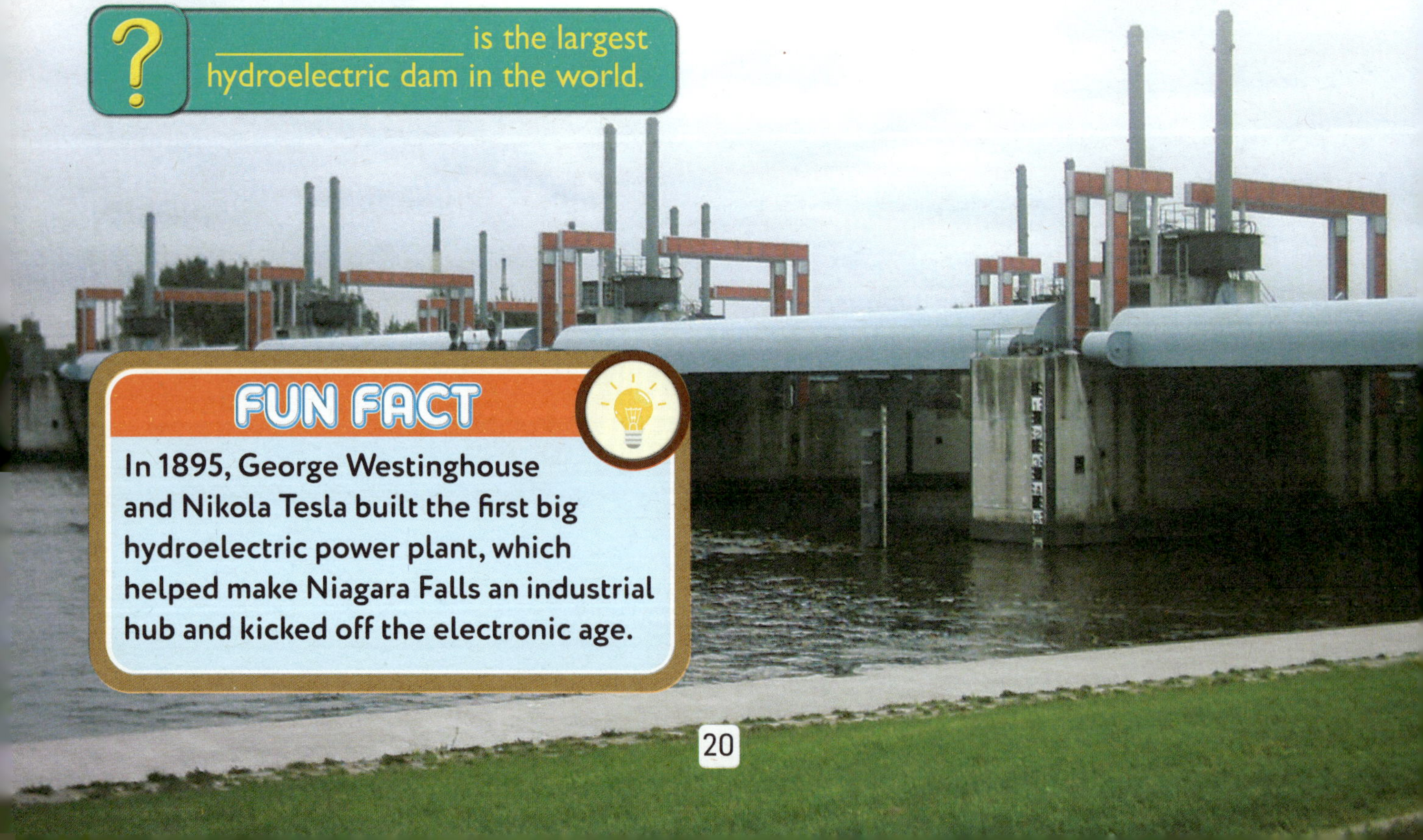

FUN FACT

In 1895, George Westinghouse and Nikola Tesla built the first big hydroelectric power plant, which helped make Niagara Falls an industrial hub and kicked off the electronic age.

Viability of Hydropower

Many nations have come to appreciate the potential of hydropower. Nevertheless, there has been considerable debate regarding its viability and environmental impact. It's worth noting that the generation of hydroenergy also contributes to the release of methane, a potent greenhouse gas.

Positives

Hydropower is the most cost-effective renewable source for electricity production. The only initial expense is the construction of a dam. Water is consistently replenished on Earth through rainfall and snowfall. Additionally, electricity production in dams is automated, eliminating labor costs.

Drawbacks

Though dams and reservoirs don't burn fuels, their warming impact can exceed even the dirtiest fossil fuel plants generating similar electricity quantities. When a reservoir is flooded, trees and plant matter settle at the bottom, decomposing without oxygen and releasing significant amounts of methane. It's estimated that the world's large dams contribute over 4 percent to global warming caused by human activities.

? ________ generates all of its electricity from renewable sources.

Solution

Scientists are aiming to transform this drawback into an advantage by extracting methane from reservoirs and utilising it as fuel in thermoelectric plants to generate additional electricity. Approximately one million tonnes of methane can produce around 1,760 megawatts of electricity.

FUN FACT

Paraguay generates all of its electricity from renewable sources, primarily hydropower.

Hydrogen Energy

Hydrogen, a primary element of the universe, can be utilised to generate power and heat with minimal or zero emissions. It is obtained from various sources including fossil fuels, natural gas, biomass, nuclear, and renewable sources.

Hydrogen Fuel Cells

Hydrogen fuel cells convert the chemical energy stored in hydrogen into electricity, powering various vehicles including personal cars, trucks, buses, marine vessels, as well as specialty vehicles like lift trucks and ground support equipment.

Types of Fuel Cells

Over time, scientists have developed different types of fuel cells for various uses. The polymer electrolyte membrane (PEM) fuel cell powers automobiles and stationary applications, while the direct-methanol fuel cell (DMFC) is ideal for portable electronic devices like laptops and battery chargers. Other types include alkaline fuel cells, phosphoric acid fuel cells, and molten carbonate fuel cells, each used in different applications.

FUN FACT

Sir William Grove, a Welsh physicist, invented the first simple hydrogen fuel cell in 1842.

? Fuel cells can be used to power trucks and buses. (True/False)

Edge Over Fossil Fuels

Fuel cells convert chemical energy into electricity, releasing only oxygen and heat as by-products, which are environmentally harmless. Hence, hydrogen fuel cells are pollution-free. However, the challenge lies in developing technology to harness hydrogen from renewable sources like solar and wind. Currently, most hydrogen is extracted from fossil fuels.

Biofuels

Biofuels are transportation fuels derived from biomass, such as sugarcane, corn, soybeans, algae, and others. They can be blended with petroleum fuels like gasoline or used independently. Biofuels are cleaner burning, emitting minimal air pollutants, though they generally cost more than fossil fuels.

What are they Made of?

Biofuels and fossil fuels are sometimes conflated because both are composed of decaying plant or animal matter. However, the crucial difference lies in their origins: biofuels are derived from recently deceased plants, while fossil fuels, like coal, originate from plants and animals buried deep within the earth for thousands of years.

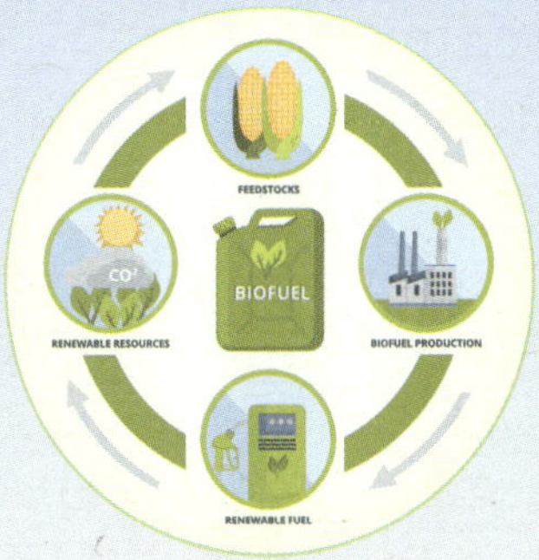

Biofuels: Past and Present

Biofuels have a long history, dating back to primitive times when wood was used for fire and cooking. In the 1850s, ethanol was utilised as a lightning fuel, and its use increased during the Second World War when fossil fuel resources became scarce. Today, ethanol is blended with gasoline to power cars and trucks, and it's also used in small engines like lawn mowers and chainsaws.

FUN FACT

Rudolf Diesel used peanut oil to run his diesel engine.

? Fossil fuels are more expensive then biofuels. (True or False)

Types of Biofuels

Ethanol and biodiesel are the primary biofuels in use. Biodiesel, mainly derived from soybean oil, can directly replace diesel fuel. Ethanol, a clear and colourless fuel, is produced from sugars found in crops like corn, barley, and sorghum, as well as from materials like potato skins, sugarcane, and rice. Both biodiesel and ethanol are rapidly growing alternative fuels globally.

Biodiesel

Biodiesel emits fewer air pollutants and boasts excellent lubricating properties, making it an ideal transportation fuel. It can also be blended with petroleum diesel, known as B20 (20% biodiesel, 80% petroleum). However, both pure biodiesel and B20 are sensitive to cold temperatures and require careful transportation.

Ethanol

Unlike gasoline, pure ethanol is nontoxic and can be used as a transportation fuel by blending it with gasoline. A common blend is E10, consisting of 10 percent ethanol and 90 percent gasoline. E85, containing about 85 percent ethanol, is used in Flexible Fuel Vehicles (FFVs). However, ethanol, like gasoline, is highly flammable and requires special precautions during transportation.

Reduce Warming

Using biodiesel or ethanol instead of petroleum fuels for transportation can greatly reduce greenhouse gas emissions from vehicles. Although biofuels still emit carbon dioxide and other gases, the amount is significantly lower than that released by fossil fuels. Moreover, biofuels are renewable, as more crops can be grown to produce them.

? Pure biodiesel is sensitive to hot temperatures. (Yes/No)

FUN FACT

When biodiesel burns, it smells like French fries.

Glossary

Acid rain: rain containing high levels of acid that is damaging to the environment.

Automate: the process of using machines to perform work to save human effort.

Biomass: plant and animal substances used for fuel.

Boon: something that brings great benefits.

Coastal: situated near the land beside a sea.

Concentration: the amount of a substance present in something.

Conventional: usual or traditional.

Decompose: to decay by a slow natural process.

Dilemma: a situation in which a difficult decision has to be made.

Drill: to make a hole in something.

Drought: a long period of time when there is little or no rain, causing crops to die.

Efficient: working well and producing good results by using available energy effectively.

Emission: the act of releasing gas or heat into the air.

Generating capacity: the amount of power which a power plant can produce at a time.

Gravitation: the force of attraction between all the masses in the universe.

Harness: to bring under control for effective use.

Harvest: to collect something, typically crops.

Heatwave: a very long period of excessively hot weather.

Hurdle: a barrier or an obstacle.

Hurricane: a severe cyclone with a wind speed exceeding 70 miles per hour, accompanied by heavy rain and lightning.

Industrial revolution: a period from the late 1700s to the early 1800s when machines were used for all work.

Insulate: to cover with a material that prevents leakage or the transfer of heat.

Irreversible: impossible to change.

Kayaking: a water sport involving water travel in a small boat using a paddle to move forward.

Mechanical: operated by a system of machines.

Offshore: in the sea; not on land.

Precipitation: rain, snow, or hail.

Prehistoric: relating to a period of time when events were not recorded.

Replenish: to bring something back to its previous levels by filling it up again.

Reverse: to turn to an opposite situation.

Salinity: containing salt.

Turbine: a machine with blades rotated by the pressure of steam, air, or water.

Water skiing: a sport in which one stands on skis and rides on the surface of water while being pulled behind a boat.

Answers

Page 7 - Coal beds
Page 8 - 80 to 85 percent
Page 9 - Bhadla Solar Park
Page 10 - mobile phones
Page 11 - True
Page 12 - Internal
Page 13 - lasers
Page 14 - Professor James Blyth
Page 15 - True
Page 16 - Larderello, Italy
Page 17 - The United States
Page 18 - Sihwa lake power plant
Page 19 - Oscillating water column (OWC)
Page 20 - The Three Gorges Dam
Page 21 - Paraguay
Page 22 - True
Page 23 - False
Page 24 - No

REUSING AND RECYCLING

Introduction

Global warming poses a significant threat to our environment and existence. Human activities have caused major climate changes, including rising global temperatures, melting polar ice sheets and caps, increased sea levels, and abnormal evaporation and precipitation.

One significant threat to the climate stems from the vast waste generated by humans. This waste directly contributes to greenhouse gas (GHG) emissions and resource wastage.

To mitigate this, reducing and recycling solid waste actively reduces GHG emissions by preventing waste from ending up in landfills, where it generates GHGs. The manufacture, distribution, use, and management of waste from products also contribute to GHG emissions.

Impact of Waste

Any unwanted or useless material that we discard is considered waste. The significant volumes of trash or garbage we dispose of directly and indirectly contribute to global warming. Our waste generation is closely associated with the emission of greenhouse gases (GHGs).

GHGs

CO_2 and methane are two potent GHGs generated during waste generation. CO_2, the most abundant GHG in the atmosphere, is directly produced when fuels are burnt to generate energy. Methane is produced during the decomposition of organic waste, including wood, paper, and food waste.

Zero Waste

Reducing waste generation and minimising our carbon footprint can help overcome the threat of global warming. The substantial GHG emissions associated with the production, consumption, and disposal of goods highlight the need to adopt environmentally friendly practices.

Climate Change

An elevated concentration of CO_2 and methane in the atmosphere leads to global climate change by trapping the sun's heat, resulting in rising global temperatures. This phenomenon causes polar ice sheets to melt, endangering low-lying regions worldwide with the risk of submersion due to rising sea levels.

FUN FACT

The United States is the world's top trash-producing nation, with each person generating 1,609 pounds of trash annually.

? Which country is the top producer of trash in the world? ______________

Product Generation

Large-scale production of goods consumes significant resources and energy. Each product's manufacturing process involves energy, material inputs, and waste generation. Discarding products wastes the energy and resources invested in their manufacturing.

Use of Energy

Every stage in a product's life cycle, from obtaining raw materials to manufacturing, requires energy, often derived from fuels like coal, petroleum, and diesel. These processes release various greenhouse gases into the atmosphere.

FUN FACT

The methane released from coal mines accounts for 8% of global methane emissions.

Raw Material

Man's destruction of natural environments and deforestation for raw material extraction contribute significantly to global warming. Mining activities, particularly for metals, emit toxic gases like sulphur dioxide. Similarly, the extraction of coal and oil also releases various harmful gases into the atmosphere.

Distribution

Fuel-powered trucks and vehicles are utilised for distributing raw materials and finished products, resulting in the emission of greenhouse gases (GHGs) like CO (carbon monoxide) and CO_2. Additionally, packaging products for distribution contributes to significant waste generation.

? Carbon monoxide is a GHG. (True or False)

Landfills

The majority of waste we generate ends up in landfills—large pits in the ground for dumping waste. They are carefully constructed, and waste is separated and compressed to avoid any interaction with groundwater and the atmosphere. However, as the waste stored in landfills decomposes, it releases many harmful gases.

Harnessing Landfill Gas

Efforts are underway to reduce the environmental impact of greenhouse gases (GHGs). Methane, a potent GHG, is converted to CO_2 through flaring to lessen its impact on global warming. Methane emitted from landfills is also recovered for heating and electricity generation. Gas-to-energy projects aim to utilize landfill gas for electricity generation, thus minimising harmful effects.

Harmful Effects

Toxic water seeping through landfills frequently leaks, contaminating groundwater resources. In 2005, gases emitted from wastewater treatment and landfills accounted for 2.3% of GHG emissions in the US.

Landfill Gas

Methane constitutes approximately 40-60 percent of landfill gas, with 35 percent being CO_2. Methane is highly inflammable and contributes to global warming. Landfill gas also contains traces of water vapour, oxygen, nitrogen, sulphur, and other contaminants.

FUN FACT

Methane traps 30 times more heat than CO_2, contributing to 18% more energy.

? How much methane is present in landfill gas? ____________

Combustion of Solid Waste

Much of our waste is disposed of in incinerators, large furnaces designed for burning. While incineration is a common method for managing solid waste, unsafe practices can harm the atmosphere.

Combustion of Solid Waste

Many people burn solid waste without realizing its harmful effects. Uncontrolled burning releases harmful gases like CO_2 and CO. Chemicals, hydrocarbons, and sulphur compounds in the waste also emit toxic gases, posing risks to the environment and public health.

CO_2

Burning organic matter like coal, oil, and wood converts solid carbon into CO_2. When a tonne of organic waste is burned, it produces the same amount of CO_2 as in landfills. Therefore, incinerating solid wastes generates more CO_2 than landfills.

? ______________ is also known as laughing gas.

Nitrous Oxide

The combustion of solid waste, sewage treatment, and agricultural processes produce another greenhouse gas known as nitrous oxide, a major air pollutant that contributes to the depletion of the ozone layer, allowing harmful ultraviolet rays from the sun to reach the earth.

FUN FACT

Nitrous oxide, also known as "laughing gas," induces euphoric effects when inhaled.

Biodegradable Waste

Biodegradable waste, originating from living organisms, easily decomposes in natural conditions. Examples include food waste, paper waste, plant and crop waste, manure, sewage, wood, and timber. When disposed of in landfills, it emits large amounts of methane gas.

Composting process

Compost is created by mixing various organic wastes together and allowing them to decompose in the presence of oxygen. This process involves the breakdown of waste materials by worms, insects, bacteria, and fungi. As these organisms consume the organic waste, it decomposes and transforms into a sweet-smelling humus. The mixture includes elements such as air, water, carbon, and nitrogen.

Biogas

Anaerobic digestion, the breakdown of organic material by microorganisms without oxygen, produces biogas, primarily methane and CO_2. This process efficiently converts waste into energy, mitigating its impact on global warming.

Benefits of Composting

Composting prevents biodegradable waste from reaching landfills, serving as nature's recycling method. It produces humus, a nutrient-rich fertiliser for gardens and parks, reducing reliance on chemical fertilisers and preserving natural resources.

? What process is used to generate biogas? ______________

Composting and Greenhouse Effect

Composting also helps to reduce GHG emissions. While many people believe that disposing of food scraps and paper products in landfills is harmless because these materials are biodegradable, they actually decompose without oxygen in landfills, releasing methane, a gas more potent than CO_2.

FUN FACT

Every pound of solid waste deposited in a landfill leads to the emission of two pounds of greenhouse gases (GHGs).

Reduce

To tackle global warming, it's vital to adopt the three Rs of waste management: reduce, reuse, and recycle. Start by minimizing consumption to decrease waste production, fostering a cleaner environment.

Buy Less

To minimize waste, we should prioritise purchasing essential, durable, and reusable items. It's important to utilise everything we buy and avoid overbuying food beyond consumption capacity.

Packaging

To avoid waste, opt for items with reusable or recyclable packaging, and purchase products like shampoos and detergents in larger quantities or bulk to reduce packaging waste.

Avoid Disposable Products

Whenever possible, opt for reusable items over disposable ones. Disposable plates and utensils can linger in landfills for extended periods. Using reusable bags for shopping helps reduce the amount of plastic waste that ends up polluting our water bodies.

Save Resources

We should adopt simple practices like turning off lights and taps when not in use and powering down electronics when not needed. While these actions may not directly reduce waste, they help conserve energy resources and avoid air pollution.

FUN FACT

An energy-smart clothes washer can save more water in one year than one person drinks in an entire lifetime.

? Should we use reusable items? ______________________

Reuse

Reusing items is a powerful waste prevention method. It involves discovering new purposes for waste items, reducing the need for disposal and conserving significant landfill space.

Donate

Unused clothing or unnecessary items can be donated to those in need or sold through backyard sales or charities. This includes old furniture, electronic appliances, and other items that are of little use to us.

FUN FACT

Glass is infinitely recyclable and also doesn't impact the flavor or freshness of food or drinks.

Repair

Consider repairing or mending broken toys, torn clothes, worn-out shoes, and electronic appliances before discarding them. Exploring all reuse possibilities can reduce waste sent to landfills and contribute to environmental sustainability.

Alternative Uses

Waste items have multiple reuse possibilities. Old clothes can become cleaning rags, plastic bags can serve as garbage bins, and newspapers can be used for packaging. Empty containers are ideal for refilling, and wastewater finds applications in industries, parks watering, and car washes.

? What should we do with broken toys, tools or torn clothes? ____________

Recycle

Recycling is the process of reusing waste to create new products, reducing the amount of garbage sent to landfills and cutting down on the extraction of raw materials from the earth.

What can be recycled?

Glass, paper, plastic, and aluminum are widely recycled materials. Additionally, batteries, biodegradable waste, concrete, electronics, and steel can also undergo recycling.

Separation at Source

Separating recyclable materials at the source is essential for efficient recycling. It's important to differentiate between biodegradable and non-biodegradable items and to avoid mixing hazardous waste with regular waste.

FUN FACT

Around 60% of the waste in landfills can be composted or recycled.

Recycling loop

The three arrows in a recycling logo represent the three recycling processes: collection, recycling, and resale. Waste is collected, processed, and turned into new products, closing the loop when consumers purchase these recycled items. A recycling symbol on a product indicates it's made from recycled material or is recyclable.

? What do the three arrows in the recycle logo signify? ____________________

Recycling Paper

Every day, we use large amounts of paper for various purposes like writing, drawing, printing, and packaging. However, the paper we throw away contributes significantly to global warming. Made from cellulose, a plant material, paper accounts for about 33% of household waste.

Conserving Forests

Paper recycling saves trees and reduces energy usage. Recycling one tonne of paper preserves about 17 trees and 3,000 gallons of water. Preserving trees ensures a healthier environment as they absorb CO_2 and release oxygen. Additionally, it prevents habitat destruction caused by deforestation for paper production.

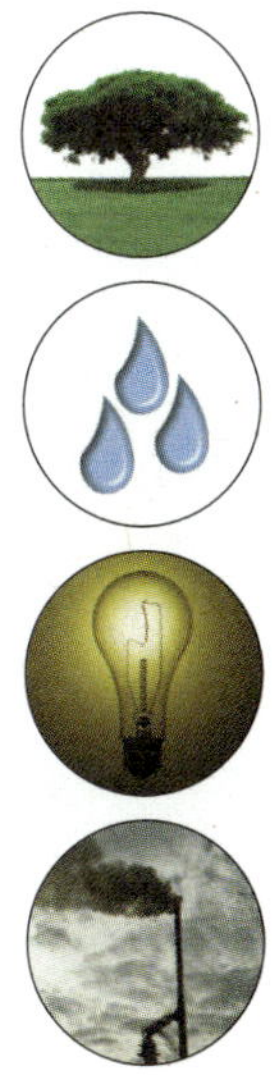

Recycled Products

Recycled paper finds use in various products like copier paper, paper towels, napkins, and toilet paper. The recycling symbol on items such as cereal boxes and notebook paper signifies their production from recycled fibre.

FUN FACT

Wood fiber can only be recycled up to five times before it becomes too weak for further recycling.

Preventing Global Warming

Recycling paper consumes 60% less energy than producing paper from fresh pulp, conserving fossil fuels. Additionally, it decreases water pollution by 35% and air pollution by 74%, while also preventing toxic pollutants from harming the environment. Paper in landfills generates methane gas.

? _________ trees are saved by recycling one tonne of paper.

Glass Recycling

Glass waste, including broken glass, bottles, and other items, poses a significant risk of injury to waste handlers and rag pickers. Once in landfills, glass can remain intact for over 4,000 years. However, glass can be recycled numerous times without any loss in quality or purity.

Recycling Benefits

Recycling a glass bottle can save enough energy to power a computer for half an hour. It also reduces air pollution by 20% and water pollution by 50%. Producing one tonne of glass from waste saves 174 kg of mining waste and results in 315 kg less CO_2 emissions.

Collection of Used Glass

Various collection schemes and glass disposal programs have been implemented to prevent glass from ending up in the garbage. In several countries, offering refunds for returned glass bottles has encouraged recycling.

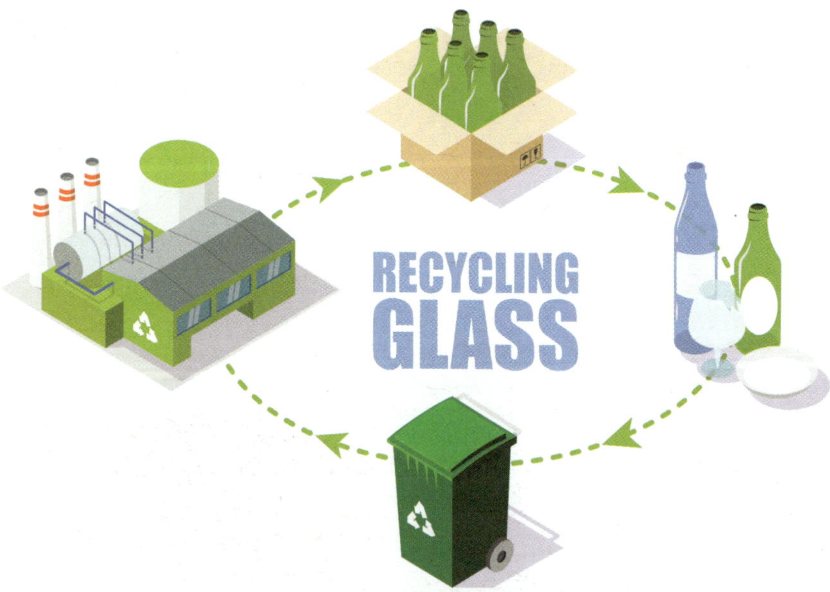

Can crystals and mirrors be recycled? ______________

Glass Recycle Process

Waste glass is cleaned to remove impurities, then melted into cullets. These cullets are sold to glass bottle manufacturers, who use them along with soda ash and limestone to make new glass containers. Recycling glass into new bottles takes only 30 days. Recycled glass is also used for fibreglass insulation, countertops, tiles, and road construction materials.

FUN FACT

Pyrex, mirrors, and crystal are not recyclable.

Steel Recycling

Steel is highly valued for its strength, quality, and durability, making it one of the most widely used materials globally. It is extensively utilised in road construction, building infrastructure, and various applications such as vehicles, surgical equipment, and household appliances.

Usage

Steel's strength makes it a popular choice for construction projects. Steel containers are versatile, able to store various products like food, paint, or shoe polish. They only require rinsing before recycling.

Benefits of Recycling Steel

Steel recycling, relying on scrap metal as its main raw material, consumes 75% less energy compared to steel production from iron ore. This saved energy can power 18 million homes. One tonne of recycled steel conserves 1,133 kg of iron ore, 635 kg of coal, and 54 kg of limestone. By recycling steel, the need for additional iron and coal mining is avoided.

Steel Recycling

Steel recycling conserves landfill space and supplies scrap to the steel industry. Recycled steel retains the same strength as new steel in applications like car parts and household appliances. Unlike other materials, steel doesn't require sorting by colour or size before recycling; it can all be melted down together.

FUN FACT

The annual amount of wood and paper waste we discard could heat 50 million homes for 20 years.

? Recycled steel has the same strength as new steel. (True or False)

Aluminum Recycling

Aluminum, a lightweight metal widely used in beverage can production due to its durability and flexibility, stands as the most recycled consumer product in the US. Additionally, items like siding, foil, car parts, and lawn furniture can also undergo recycling. Notably, aluminum is entirely recyclable and can be reused indefinitely.

Benefits

An aluminium can in a landfill will remain for nearly 500 years before breaking down. Recycling aluminium produces enough energy to power a TV for three hours. Burning an aluminium can releases numerous toxic gases. Recycling 45 aluminium cans can save up to 3.78 litres of crude oil used in production. Producing recycled aluminium requires 95% less energy than deriving it from bauxite ore, resulting in reduced carbon emissions.

Recycling Process

We use over 80 billion aluminum soda cans annually. After discarding, these cans are cleaned and melted at high temperatures, forming ingots. These ingots are sent to can sheet manufacturers who produce cans and sell them to beverage industries. The recycling process for aluminum cans takes less than 60 days, ensuring they return to stores quickly.

FUN FACT

Americans discard approximately 40 million beverage cans. If placed end-to-end, these cans could stretch to the moon and back nearly 20 times.

? How long does it take one aluminum can to decompose? ____________

E-waste

E-waste includes outdated electronics like computers, kitchen appliances, cell phones, and TVs that are no longer useful. Rapid technological advancements lead to short lifespans for electronic devices, prompting quick replacements with newer models.

Threat to Environment

Improper e-waste disposal threatens the environment, as electronic devices contain toxic chemicals like lead, mercury, and cadmium. Much e-waste is sent to landfills, incinerators, or illegally exported to developing countries. Burning e-waste to retrieve metals releases toxic gases. Information technology contributes 2% to global warming, says an IT research company.

Corporate Programmes

To address the e-waste problem, companies like Apple, Dell, Whirlpool, and Sony have launched recycling schemes. Sony has established 'drop-off centres' in its retail stores for recycling its products. Nokia also encourages customers to return old handsets through a similar programme.

Recycling E-waste

Only 15% of yearly e-waste is recycled. Recycling one million desktop computers properly can cut GHG emissions equivalent to the yearly emissions of over 17,000 cars. Often, only some parts of electronic appliances are recycled, with the rest being dumped. Careful handling is needed when recycling electronic devices to extract components like glass, copper, aluminium, and plastic.

FUN FACT

Our e-waste extends beyond Earth in the form of non-working satellites drifting in space. Efforts are underway to recycle these satellites.

? E-waste is illegally exported to developing countries for _______.

Construction & Demolition Waste

Construction and demolition generates large quantities of waste, often called C&D waste. This waste is a mixture of clay, concrete, timber, stone, tiles, cement, steel, glass, shingles, and other materials. Construction waste may also include toxic substances like asbestos and lead.

Contribution to Global Warming

C&D waste contributes directly to global warming by releasing greenhouse gases (GHGs) into the atmosphere. This waste includes significant amounts of timber, cardboard, metal, and concrete. Wood and other construction waste are major sources of methane gas emissions from landfills. Additionally, building activities generate hazardous wastes like asbestos.

Recycling C&D Waste

C&D waste can dominate landfill space, but recycling it alleviates this pressure and conserves energy needed for new material production. Recycling concrete and asphalt for road construction, using soil as landfill covers, and repurposing wood and timber from demolition sites are effective strategies. Plastics, glass, and metals can be sent to dedicated recycling facilities.

FUN FACT

Recycling C&D waste can help conserve finite resources, prevent increased use of landfills, and maximise the lifespan of materials.

?

Asphalt can be reused. (True or False)

Reuse and Recycle Clothes

Textile waste includes fabric items like clothes, bedding, shoes, and soft toys, made of fibres such as cotton, nylon, wool, linen, and flannel. Over a million tonnes of textile waste come from households annually, with garment manufacturers and retail industries also contributing.

Recycling Benefits

Textiles pose significant dumping challenges, especially synthetic fibres, which resist decomposition and persist in landfills for millennia. Conversely, natural fabrics like wool and cotton decompose more easily, albeit producing methane gas. Recycling textiles mitigates pollution by conserving resources and reducing reliance on imported raw materials.

Reuse

Textile waste offers numerous reuse opportunities. It can be repaired and repurposed as rags for paint stores, machine shops, and industries, or donated to those in need. Alternatively, it can be sold at jumbo sales or online platforms, lessening the strain on landfills. Additionally, textile waste can be utilized for creating upholstery in new homes, further extending its lifespan.

Recycle

According to the UK Environment Agency, about 97% of textiles can be recycled. Recycling textiles is energy-efficient and produces no harmful byproducts. Materials are sorted by quality, type, and condition. Wearable items are often sold to Third World countries, while unwearable textiles are shredded for use in car insulation, furniture fillings, and panel linings. Buttons and zippers are stripped for reuse.

? Synthetic fibres decompose easily. (True or False)

FUN FACT

Only 8% of old clothes are reused, and 10% are recycled

Plastic Recycling

Plastic is a versatile, lightweight, durable, and cost-effective material. It's used to make various products including food containers, pipes, shopping bags, bottle crates, sacks, water pipes, windscreen wipers, and more.

Threat to Environment

Natural resources like crude oil, natural gas, and oil are essential for plastic production. Once depleted, these resources cannot be replaced. Since most plastics are non-biodegradable, they persist in the environment for thousands of years. Moreover, both the production and disposal of plastics generate significant amounts of greenhouse gases (GHGs).

Labelled Plastics

Not all plastic materials are recyclable. Plastic products are labelled with a number indicating the material they're made of, helping identify toxicity. Generally, plastics labelled 1, 2, and 3 are recyclable, while those labelled 4, 5, 6, and 7 are less easily recycled. Items like egg trays, cups, and plates are particularly challenging to recycle.

FUN FACT

According to the American Chemistry Council, about 8% of crude oil is used to make plastics.

? Plastic containers labelled as 1, 2, and 3 are ___________.

Plastic Recycling Process

Used plastic bottles and containers are collected, washed, and inspected before being cut into small pieces and melted. The melted plastic is formed into long strands, then cut into pellets for use in factories. Recycled plastic can be used to make tables, chairs, stationery, and packaging materials.

Waste Reduction

To mitigate individual contributions to global warming, different countries have adopted various methods and policies. Increased awareness about waste and its impact on global warming has led to greater responsibility among businesses and individuals worldwide.

'Pay as You Throw' Programmes

Some communities implement waste charging schemes where residents pay fees based on the amount of waste they produce. This fee covers the disposal of local solid waste, measured by size and weight. Such schemes incentivize residents to reduce waste and increase recycling efforts.

Plastic Bags

Plastic bags are globally produced and take thousands of years to decompose due to their material mix. They litter streets and waterways, endanger wildlife, and contribute to climate change. To address this, several countries and regions have banned single-use plastic shopping bags, instead charging customers for their use.

Waste Collection

Separating waste at the point of disposal helps prevent biodegradable and hazardous waste from ending up in landfills. Public places feature bins of different colours, educating consumers on proper disposal methods for food waste, non-biodegradable waste, and hazardous materials. Over 75% of the house hold waste is recyclable, but only 30% of it is recycled

? Over __________ of the household waste can be recycled.

FUN FACT

12 million tonnes of plastic finds its way into the ocean every single year.

Animal Waste

Animal farming and cattle rearing significantly contribute to global climate change. The production of meat, eggs, and milk involves not only raising and slaughtering animals but also grain production for animal feed. Additionally, the waste produced by these animals, along with its disposal and storage, contributes to global warming.

Animal Rearing

Approximately 56 billion land animals are raised and slaughtered for human consumption each year. Farm animals and production facilities occupy one-third of the planet's land surface, leading to deforestation, land degradation, and increased CO_2 emissions. Overgrazing by farm animals further depletes wooded areas.

Animal Waste and GHGs

The animal agriculture sector emits 35-40% of annual methane, with ruminants such as sheep, goats, and cows producing methane during digestion. Cattle raised for dairy products are fed high-protein diets of corn and soybeans, leading to increased greenhouse gas emissions. Untreated animal waste pollutes nearby water bodies.

FUN FACT

The animal agriculture sector accounts for about 9% of the total CO_2 emissions.

Trash to Treasure

Animal feces and manure release large amounts of GHGs. Efforts are being made to recycle animal waste into fuel. Methane from animal manure can heat homes, cook meals, and generate electricity. Rotting waste produces methane and N_2O by bacteria action. Dry-stacked manure is used in agricultural soil, producing minimal methane.

? How many land animals are reared and slaughtered for human consumption annually? ____________

Glossary

Asbestos: a fire-resistant mineral used in fabric and materials.

Asphalt: a sticky substance used in road construction.

Bauxite: an ore that yields aluminum metal.

Biodegradable: substances that can be broken down by bacteria, posing no harm to the environment.

Cadmium: a metallic element found in batteries.

Carbon footprint: the amount of CO_2 emitted by a person, organisation, or building.

Combustion: the process of burning.

Compost: decaying plants and animals used as fertilizer.

Compress: to press or squeeze something.

Contaminant: a substance that pollutes or makes something dirty.

Corrugated: material shaped into parallel folds.

Countertop: a flat surface in kitchens or bathrooms.

Deplete: to reduce the amount of something.

Disposable: designed to be thrown away after use.

Economic: related to business, industry, and trade.

Faeces: solid waste from humans and animals.

Flannel: soft cotton fabric used for clothing.

Fuel cell: a power-producing cell in electric vehicles.

Habitat: the natural home of an organism.

Incineration: burning something completely.

Landfill: a large hole where waste is buried.

Ore: a solid material from which metals or minerals are extracted.

Organic: related to living matter.

Ream: a large quantity of something.

Retail: pertaining to the sale of goods directly to the public for personal use.

Ruminant: an animal that regurgitates food from its stomach to chew again.

Scrap: a small amount of leftover food after a meal.

Sewage: wastewater and excrement removed from buildings via underground pipes.

Shingle: small, rounded pebbles.

Slaughter: the act of killing animals, typically for meat.

Toxic: poisonous and harmful to people, animals, and the environment.

Turbine: an engine or machine that generates power using liquid or gas pressure on a wheel.

Upholstery: fabric used to cover chairs and sofas.

Answers

Page 29 - USA
Page 30 - True
Page 31 - 40-60%
Page 32 - Nitrous oxide
Page 33 - Anaerobic digestion
Page 34 - Yes
Page 35 - Repair them for reuse
Page 36 - Collection, recycling, resale
Page 37 - 17
Page 38 - No
Page 39 - True
Page 40 - 500 years
Page 41 - Recycling
Page 42 - True
Page 43 - False
Page 44 - Recyclable
Page 45 - Two thirds
Page 46 - Approximately 56 billion

SAVE ENERGY

Introduction

A significant portion of electricity and fuels is produced by burning fossil fuels, releasing harmful greenhouse gases (GHGs) that contribute to global warming. Saving energy is crucial to reduce these emissions. Additionally, fossil fuels are nonrenewable and finite. With their depletion inevitable in the near future, it's essential to explore alternative energy sources.

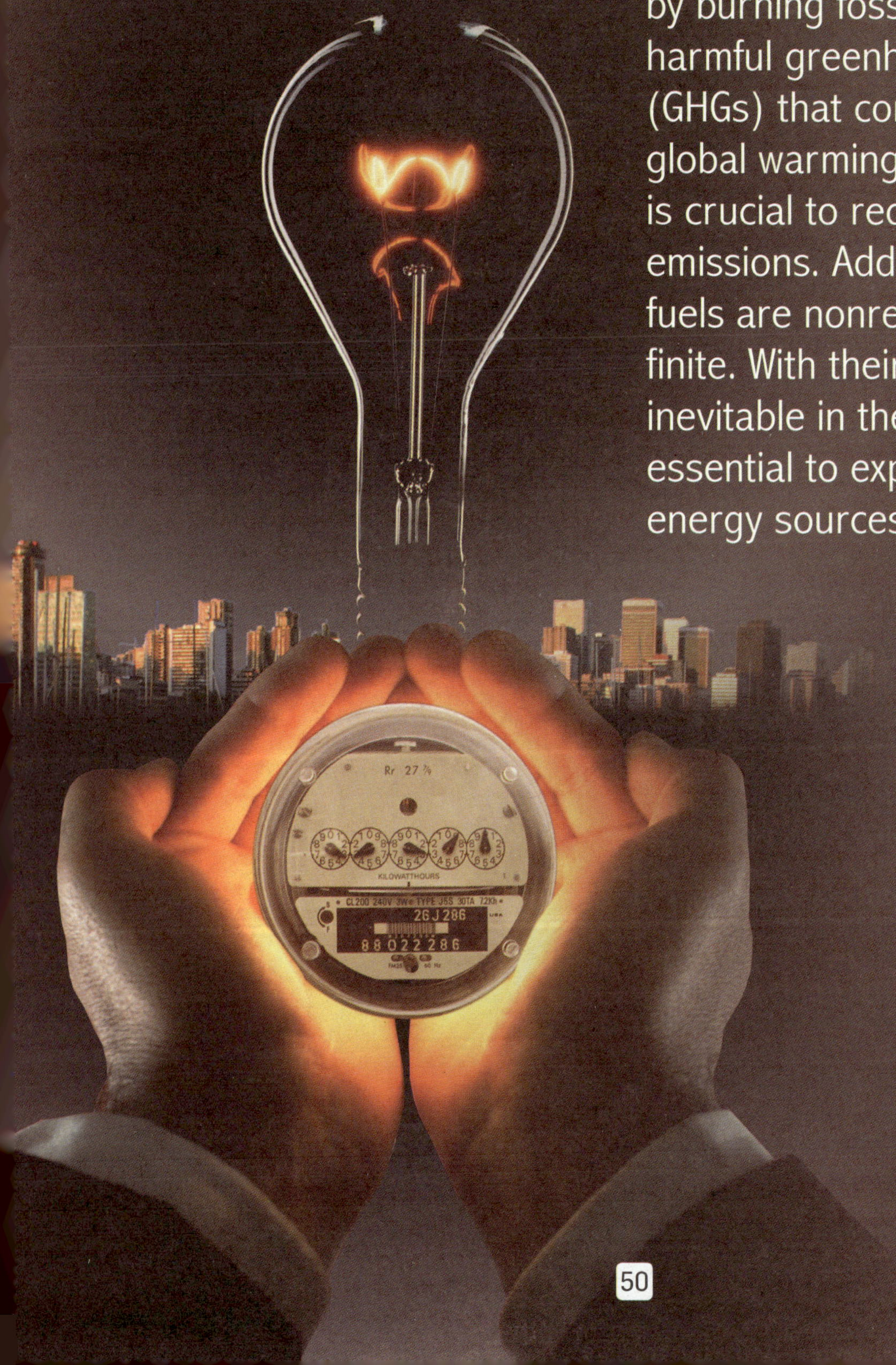

What is Energy?

Energy is the capacity for work, essential for illuminating homes, powering vehicles, and fueling industries. Historically, fossil fuels became widely employed for these purposes. Yet, excessive reliance on them exacerbates global warming.

Sources of Energy

Energy is sourced diversely and serves various purposes. Living organisms harness energy from the sun as heat and light. Inanimate objects such as machinery and vehicles derive energy from fuels like gasoline, diesel, and electricity.

Gasoline and Diesel

Globally, gasoline and diesel fuel most vehicles, derived from crude oil refining in oil refineries. However, these refineries emit significant greenhouse gases, exacerbating global warming. To combat this, conserving energy and seeking alternatives to these readily transportable fuels is imperative.

Electricity

Electricity, the primary energy source, has been integral to daily life for centuries, powering appliances like washing machines and TVs. While traditionally generated from fossil fuels, pollution concerns and dwindling resources prompt a shift towards hydropower, wind, solar, and nuclear energy.

FUN FACT

Energy cannot be destroyed; it merely changes forms.

? Electricity is a form of energy. (True/False)

Sources of Energy

Renewable and nonrenewable are the two types of sources that produce usable forms of energy. Nonrenewable sources cannot be replenished quickly, while renewable sources can be reproduced through natural processes.

Fossil Fuels

Natural gas, coal, and crude oil are fossil fuels, widely used as non-renewable energy sources. These fuels originated over 300 million years ago, formed by the earth's core heat and pressure acting on the remains of deceased plants and animals.

Renewable Sources

There are five types of renewable energy sources:

- **Solar energy:** derived from the sun's heat and light.
- **Hydro energy:** generated from the kinetic energy of water.
- **Wind energy:** harnessed from strong winds.
- **Geothermal energy:** produced from the earth's heat.
- **Biomass energy:** obtained from plants and trees. Fuels like ethanol and biodiesel are made from corn and vegetable oil, respectively.

Uranium (nuclear energy)

Uranium, an element, serves as another nonrenewable energy source. Energy is generated through nuclear fission, a process where uranium atoms split. This method is cleaner compared to fossil fuels, albeit expensive.

FUN FACT

All fossil fuels were formed during the Carboniferous Period, spanning approximately from 360 to 286 million years ago.

? Nuclear energy is derived from ____________.

Electricity Generation

Fossil fuels, nuclear energy, solar power, wind, water, and biomass are the primary energy sources. When converted into more usable forms, they become secondary sources. Fossil fuels particularly play a significant role in powering electricity generation, upon which we heavily rely.

Thermal Power Stations

In thermal power plants, electricity is produced by burning coal. The combustion heats water in the boiler, creating steam. This steam drives a turbine connected to a generator, generating electricity. However, coal burning releases significant CO2 emissions into the atmosphere. Despite this, thermal power plants remain the primary electricity source in many countries worldwide.

Other Power Stations

To combat global warming, it's imperative to generate electricity through methods that don't emit harmful GHGs:

- **Solar power plants:** Convert solar energy into electricity using technologies like solar cells and panels.
- **Hydroelectric power plants:** Generate electricity by utilizing water flow to turn turbines connected to electric generators at dams.
- **Nuclear power plants:** Produce heat through nuclear fission, where uranium atoms split upon neutron impact, releasing substantial heat to spin turbines for electricity generation.
- **Wind power plants:** Harness electricity from strong winds by turning windmills connected to electric generator turbines.

FUN FACT

Approximately 20% of the world's electricity is generated in hydroelectric power plants.

? Which type of power plant uses water to generate electricity? ______________

Oil and Natural Gas Drilling

Crude oil, often termed "black gold," and natural gas, primarily methane, are valuable energy sources found underground. Extracting them incurs significant energy costs and releases pollutants into the atmosphere.

Oil Drilling

Crude oil lies in rocks deep within the Earth's layers, including the seabed. Experts analyse rock formations to locate potential oil reservoirs. Drilling demands substantial energy, with rigs equipped with electric motors and generators consuming power during extraction. Oil is then processed and transported via tankers and pipelines to refineries, also consuming energy.

Natural Gas Extraction

While natural gas is among the most environmentally friendly fossil fuels, its exploration, production, and transportation entail significant energy costs. Electric power is used to drill wells in gas fields, followed by processing at plants to remove impurities and separate components. Extensive underground pipelines are then required to transport the gas to its destination, all of which consume valuable energy.

FUN FACT

The US is the world's largest producer of natural gas.

? Gasoline is derived from crude oil. (True/False)

Arctic Oil Drilling

An estimated quarter of the Earth's undiscovered oil is believed to be located in the Arctic Circle's ocean floor. Oil companies are increasingly turning to the unspoiled waters of the Arctic Ocean for drilling. However, Arctic oil drilling poses significant risks to both native wildlife and the environment.

High Risk Enterprise

The Arctic's remote setting, freezing temperatures, and extreme weather pose significant dangers for workers. Icebergs further escalate risks in oil drilling operations. Large ships are required to maneuver icebergs, and sometimes drilling must halt to avoid massive icebergs, some city-sized, blocking the way.

Dangers

Drilling for oil in the Arctic comes with risks, including potential harm to underwater life, local Eskimo communities reliant on native animals, wildlife, and the Arctic ecosystem. In response, an oil company planning Arctic drilling has developed new technology to minimize drilling noise.

Oiled crested auket

Possibility of Oil Spill

Arctic oil drilling raises major concerns due to the risk of oil spills in frozen areas. Presently, no technology can effectively clean up such spills. The consequences would be catastrophic for local fisheries and the environment, affecting millions of migrating birds, seabird species, polar bears, seals, arctic foxes, and bowhead whales.

FUN FACT

Approximately 4 million people live in the Arctic.

? The Arctic oil spill would have devastating effects on the environment. (True/False)

Energy and Global Warming

CO2 is the primary greenhouse gas (GHG) responsible for increasing global temperatures. It's emitted significantly during electricity production, oil refining, and vehicle fuel combustion. Thus, conserving energy is crucial to reduce CO2 emissions and mitigate global warming.

Electrical Pollution

Electricity generation from burning fossil fuels in power plants contributes to air pollution, exacerbating global warming. Keeping appliances switched on when not in use leads to electrical pollution, associated with various health issues like cardiac and neurological effects.

Industrial Pollution

Since the 1700s, coal has been burned to satisfy global industrial energy demands, which have surged with the proliferation of industries. It's essential to discourage the use of packaged materials produced by industries, as their manufacturing process releases substantial amounts of greenhouse gases (GHGs).

Transport Pollution

Oil is another extensively utilized energy source, with fuel derived through refining. As the number of vehicles on the road rises, so does oil consumption. The oil-refining process emits CO2 into the air. Moreover, burning fuel in vehicles releases additional greenhouse gases alongside CO2, further contributing to global warming.

? Electrical pollution increases global warming. (True/False)

FUN FACT

About 40 percent of CO2 emissions in the US stem from electricity production.

Save Electricity

Electricity comes from both nonrenewable and renewable sources, yet the majority worldwide is generated by burning coal in thermal power plants. Saving electricity is crucial to mitigate the harmful emissions of greenhouse gases (GHGs).

Save for the Present

Currently, the global demand for electricity far exceeds its supply, with over 1.2 billion people still lacking access to it. Additionally, increasing power cuts occur due to insufficient supply.

Why Save Electricity?

Electricity generated from burning fossil fuels is the cheapest and most reliable compared to other sources. Saving electricity not only reduces electrical pollution but also lowers electricity bills.

Save for the Future

Wasting electricity means squandering valuable fossil fuels, which will deplete if consumed at the current rate. Overuse will leave future generations reliant solely on renewable sources for electricity.

FUN FACT

In 2011, the US and China consumed approximately 4.4 and 3.4 trillion kilowatt-hours of electricity, respectively.

? Everyone in the world has access to electricity. (True/False)

Save Fuel

Every day, we use fuels to power vehicles, motors, and cook food. Fuels are derived from crude oil, a nonrenewable resource. Once used, it cannot be regenerated quickly. Therefore, it is crucial to use oil judiciously and seek alternative options that are more sustainable.

Oil-dependence Costs

Over half of the world's oil reserves lie in the Middle East, giving them power to dictate oil policies. Other nations must pay the prices set by Middle Eastern countries for each barrel of oil. Saving fuel can save other countries a lot of money.

Helps Animals

The pollution from vehicle emissions harms humans and animals. While humans can seek shelter indoors, small animals suffer directly. Saving fuel is crucial for animals to breathe freely and live longer.

FUN FACT

In the US, gasoline and diesel together make up about 80% of all of the energy used for transportation.

Controls Climate Change

When fuel is burned in vehicles, harmful greenhouse gases are emitted, exacerbating global warming. Using less fuel would result in fewer emissions, ultimately aiding in controlling climate change induced by global warming.

? Saving fuel would increase our oil-dependence cost. (True/False)

A Looming Oil Crisis

Over 87% of the world's energy is generated from fossil fuels, with approximately 40% coming from oil alone. This significant reliance on oil to fulfill energy requirements, coupled with its uncontrolled consumption, suggests an imminent oil crisis.

Effects of Oil Shortage

Oil and natural gas are essential for fertilizers and pesticides. Without them, food grain production would decline. Shortages would also raise prices of manufactured goods due to transportation issues. Healthcare would suffer as medicines and plastic disposables rely on petroleum. Concerns about energy security grow, especially in oil-importing countries. The Middle East, the world's richest oil region, faces instability due to foreign interference and political manipulation.

Predictable Future

Countries like Saudi Arabia, Canada, Iraq, Iran, Kuwait, the United Arab Emirates, Russia, Venezuela, Mexico, and the US hold the world's oil reserves. Many are nearing peak production. As oil production declines and demand rises, oil-producing nations will set terms for selling oil. Oil importers will compete for limited supplies.

FUN FACT

The Middle East has enough oil to last 88 years at the present production rates.

? An oil crisis would decrease the prices of manufactured goods. (True/False)

Energy and Recycling

There's a close link between energy and the goods we use daily. Products like electronics, batteries, toys, bottles, household items such as carpets and curtains rely on energy for production, processing, and transportation. Recycling these goods is essential for conserving energy.

Recycle

Recycling prevents items from becoming waste and ending up in landfills, where burning releases harmful gases. By recycling goods, we conserve the energy used in their manufacturing and reduce harmful emissions. Products made from recycled materials require 30% less energy in their production.

Three Rs

- **Reduce:** Cut energy usage by switching off appliances when not in use and using energy-efficient products.
- **Reuse:** It's better to reuse items like glass, as it takes about 1 million years to decompose in a landfill.
- **Recycle:** Recycling creates new items from old ones using less energy than making fresh products.

? Name the three Rs.

____

FUN FACT

The energy saved in recycling a single aluminum can could power a television for three hours.

Paper Pollution

Paper production, manufacturing, and transportation demand significant energy, leading to paper pollution. Given the widespread use of paper, recycling becomes imperative to curb this pollution. Additionally, paper recycling helps reduce the excessive use of wood pulp from trees.

Paper Production

Producing one sheet of paper typically requires almost 17 watt-hours of energy (Wh). In contrast, recycled paper uses approximately 12 Wh and nearly half the water needed to make a sheet from fresh wood pulp. Recycling one tonne of paper can save up to 17 trees. However, paper production generates harmful waste products such as dimethyl sulphide, highly toxic total reduced sulphur compounds (TRS), and volatile organic compounds (VOCs) like methanol gas, posing risks to the environment.

Reduce Paper Consumption

Purchase notebooks or diaries made of recycled paper. Opt for unbleached and uncoloured paper when possible. Buy paper in bulk to reduce packaging, which also saves energy. Print only when absolutely necessary. Avoid using paper cups and instead use your own glass.

Use Both Sides

A standard medium-sized copier can copy about 50 pages per minute, using around 1,000 watts of energy. Surprisingly, this energy is equivalent to that used in producing just one sheet of paper. Hence, printing or copying on both sides of the paper is crucial to save energy and reduce paper pollution.

FUN FACT

To tackle risks in paper production, American scientists have developed a method to recycle methanol waste into methyl formate, an eco-friendly blowing agent and solvent.

? A single sheet of paper uses_____ watts of energy in production.

Trees Save Energy

Forests cover around 30% of the land surface and are essential for the biosphere. Trees provide oxygen for living organisms; a large, leafy tree can supply a day's oxygen for about four people. They also help reduce soil erosion and offer various other benefits. Hence, it's crucial that we protect them.

Trees Save Energy

Trees cool surroundings through evapotranspiration, absorbing water through roots and evaporating it through leaves' pores. Planting more trees in residential areas reduces heat and reflection. Trees provide shade, reducing solar radiation that heats buildings, cutting the need for air conditioning and electricity. In winter, trees act as windbreaks, preventing cold winds from entering homes and reducing the need for room heaters, saving energy.

Reduce Air Pollution

CO2 emitted by factories, automobiles, and the burning of fossil fuels are major contributors to air pollution. Trees play a crucial role in mitigating this pollution by absorbing CO2 through photosynthesis, thus reducing the levels of this potent greenhouse gas. Trees help clean the air by absorbing other pollutants such as sulfur oxides and nitrogen oxides.

FUN FACT

Trees are effective noise barriers and control noise pollution.

? Trees help in cutting down noise pollution. (True/False)

Save Water, Save Energy

Thermal power plants use water to generate electricity, while energy is needed to pump, treat, and transport water worldwide. Both processes release harmful gases into the atmosphere, contributing to global warming. Therefore, conserving water is essential to saving energy and reducing emissions.

Spend Less

Conserving water automatically reduces the energy used in processing and transporting it. Additionally, using water-efficient appliances that require less water reduces water bills. Therefore, saving water not only conserves energy but also saves money.

Water Labelling Systems

Water efficiency in plumbing can be achieved by managing water output in different fixtures. However, water-efficient labelling in developing countries like India is still evolving. The IAPMO, in partnership with the Indian Plumbing Association (IPA), has proposed a water-rating system called Water Efficient Products–India (WEP-I) to rate Indian plumbing fixtures, including faucets, dishwashers, and clothes washers.

FUN FACT

Approximately 60% of a household's water footprint is attributed to lawn and garden maintenance.

? By saving water we can save energy. (True/False)

Easy Ways to Save Water

- For shaving, use a mug instead of running water.
- Close faucets while soaping and rinsing clothes.
- Upgrade older toilets with water-efficient models.
- Operate automatic washing machines and dishwashers only when fully loaded.
- Water your garden during early morning or late evening to reduce evaporation.

Threat to Wildlife

Global warming is changing the breeding and reproduction patterns of almost all wildlife species. To survive, organisms are adapting to the changing environment. However, energy projects like hydroelectric dams, wind turbines, and mining disrupt wildlife and damage ecosystems.

Mining Threat

Mining disrupts nesting sites, foraging grounds, and wildlife distribution. Surface mining releases acid-forming materials, endangering reptiles, burrowing animals, and small mammals. Indian tigers face threats from extensive coal mining. Over the past five years, India has seen a surge in coal mines and coal-run power plants, impacting tiger populations in areas like Chandrapur, Maharashtra.

Loss of Habitat

Many birds and bats are injured or killed colliding with wind turbine blades. Large wind farms cause habitat loss, forcing birds to change foraging grounds and migration routes.
Birds and bats expend extra energy navigating wind farms. Slowing turbine blades during low wind speeds at night can save many birds and bats.

Dams and Power Plants

The construction and operation of hydroelectric dams worldwide endanger many marine organisms, especially fish. Dams block migration paths of ocean-going species like salmon. Water usage in nuclear and fossil power plants also harms marine animals, as many discharge untreated heated water from their once-through cooling (OTC) systems into rivers and coastal waters.

FUN FACT

Around 5,575 tigers live in India, comprising more than half of the world's tiger population.

? How many tigers live in India? ______________________

Energy Efficiency

Energy efficiency is achieved using technology that requires less energy for the same function. Many countries rate appliances through energy efficiency programmes, assigning them energy stars. The more energy stars an appliance has, the greater its efficiency.

Energy Efficient Products

- Fluorescent bulbs: Compact fluorescents use 1/3 the energy of standard bulbs, lasting 10 times longer and producing 70% less heat.
- Refrigerators: Energy Star fridges use 75% less energy than 1980s models, saving over 5,000 rupees yearly.
- Clothes Washers: Energy Star machines use 50% less energy and 18-25 gallons of water per load, compared to 40 gallons for standard washers.
- Room air conditioners: Energy Star ACs cut energy use by 20-50% and save around 700 rupees annually.
- Home electronics: Energy Star appliances use less energy. Inkjet printers are more efficient than laser ones. LCD screens use less power than CRT or plasma.

Energy Labels

Most countries use two types of energy labels: comparative and endorsement. Comparative labels allow consumers to determine energy efficiency and compare product rankings. These labels are voluntary in some countries and typically use a scale with defined efficiency categories. Endorsement labels are used for the most energy-efficient products, featuring a mark or logo indicating compliance with standards. They may provide minimal comparative information.

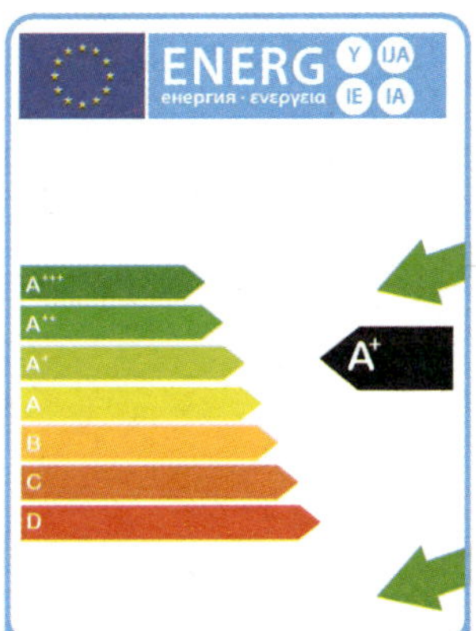

The European Union energy label

FUN FACT

Only about 10% of the energy used by a bulb creates light; the remaining 90% creates heat.

? __________ stars indicate the energy efficiency of an appliance.

Smart Meter

A smart meter is an electric meter that measures the amount of electricity used and indicates the time of day when it is used. These meters are being used in many countries like Italy, Canada, Japan, the UK, and others. Their popularity is growing worldwide.

Time-of-Use Pricing

Electricity prices vary throughout the day depending on demand and supply.

- Off-peak is when demand is low, and cheaper sources of electricity are used, typically from 7 pm to 7 am in both summers and winters.
- Mid-peak is when demand and cost are moderate, typically from 5-7 pm and 7-11 am in summers and 11 am to 5 pm in winters.
- On-peak is when demand is highest, and more expensive forms of electricity production are used, typically from 11 am to 5 pm in summers and 7-11 am and 5-7 pm in winters.

Benefits

During peak hours, electricity is sourced from nonrenewable resources, causing pollution. To reduce this, users should use electricity during mid-peak and off-peak hours when it's cheaper. Lowering consumption during peak hours can reduce bills.

FUN FACT

Italy, alongside Sweden, was among the first to roll out nationwide smart metering systems in Europe, with over 35 million customers currently using them.

? We should use most electricity during on-peak hours. (True/False)

Saving Energy at School

Young students can also join the fight against global warming. Saving energy in schools is beneficial for all of us. Schools can safeguard our future by educating students about the need and benefits of saving energy, as they would follow the same measures at their homes and elsewhere.

Energy-saving Measures

- Turn off lights when the classroom is empty.
- Use natural lighting whenever possible.
- Install 'Occupancy Sensors' to automatically turn off lights when the room is empty.
- Switch off appliances like computers and printers when not in use.
- Display awareness posters and reminder stickers next to switches.
- Close all windows when heating or cooling is on.
- Use an adjustable thermostat and adjust it according to need.

Energy Team

Energy can be saved by reducing unnecessary wastage. Teachers could establish an energy team of students to monitor the use of lights and electrical equipment in classrooms. They should report any electricity wastage to the teacher.

? For what purpose does an average school use the maximum energy?

Energy Consumption

On average, about 55% of the energy in schools is used for heating and cooling the school building. Approximately 20% is used for lighting, 15% for catering, and the remainder for computing and other purposes.

FUN FACT

Implementing energy-saving measures can help schools reduce their energy costs by approximately 20%.

Ways to Save Energy

Please check the energy-saving practices that are used at your home and start adopting the ones you don't:

- [ ] Use a programmable thermostat to adjust temperatures as needed.
- [ ] Reduce heating in unused rooms by closing doors and heat registers.
- [ ] Turn off lights when not in use to save energy.
- [ ] Close curtains and shades at night during sunny winter days; keep them open during the daytime.
- [ ] Control outdoor lights with sensor timers to prevent daytime use.
- [ ] Consider replacing gas cooking appliances with automatic electric ignition systems.
- [ ] Opt for microwave ovens, which consume 50% less energy than gas stoves.
- [ ] Turn off electric stoves several minutes before the cooking time ends.
- [ ] Use flat-bottomed pans for full contact with cooking coils.
- [ ] When cooking on gas burners, use moderate flame settings to conserve LPG.
- [ ] Utilize pressure cookers whenever possible to save energy.
- [ ] Cover pans with lids while cooking to retain heat and save energy.
- [ ] Purchase energy star-rated electrical equipment for efficiency.
- [ ] Turn off home office equipment when not in use.
- [ ] Turn off computer monitors during breaks to save power.
- [ ] Unplug battery chargers after use to prevent standby power consumption.
- [ ] Choose refrigerators/freezers with automatic moisture control for optimal performance.
- [ ] Clean refrigerator coils regularly to improve efficiency.
- [ ] Ensure refrigerator door seals are airtight to prevent energy loss.
- [ ] Minimise refrigerator door openings to conserve energy.
- [ ] Allow hot food to cool before refrigerating to reduce energy consumption.
- [ ] Thaw frozen foods in the refrigerator to save energy.
- [ ] Wash clothes in the washing machine only with full loads to maximise efficiency.
- [ ] Use cold water in the rinse cycle to save energy.
- [ ] Choose natural drying over electric dryers when possible.
- [ ] Open windows at night to cool the house during summers; close them during the day to retain cool air.
- [ ] Use air conditioners with automatic temperature cut-off for efficiency.
- [ ] Cook with a microwave to reduce heat and humidity in homes.
- [ ] Properly seal doors and windows when using AC to prevent energy loss.
- [ ] Run the dishwasher only with a full load to conserve water and energy.
- [ ] Invest in energy-efficient appliances to reduce energy consumption.
- [ ] Repair leaky faucets to prevent water and energy waste.
- [ ] Reduce water heater temperature settings to save energy.

Glossary

Avert: prevent from happening

Behavioural: relating to behaviour

Bowhead whales: Arctic whale with large mouth

Catastrophic: extremely harmful

Copier: machine for making copies

Curb: lessen intensity of

Decompose: break down

Devastating: highly destructive

Efficient: effective without waste

Employed: make use of

Endangered: in immediate danger of extinction

Exhaustible: capable of being used up

Fertilizer: substance to increase soil fertility

Fishery: workplace for catching, processing, and selling fish

Generator: engine converting mechanical to electrical energy

Greenhouse gas: gas contributing to greenhouse effect

Hygienic: clean and sanitary

Iceberg: large mass of floating ice

Impel: urge or force into action

Impending: close in time

Incessantly: without interruption

Kilowatt hour: unit of energy

Kinetic energy: energy of motion

Landfill: low area for burying waste

Migrating: moving periodically or seasonally

Neutron: elementary particle with zero charge

Oil spill: thin film of oil on water

Pesticide: chemical for killing pests

Precious: of high worth

Pristine: completely clean or pure

Refinery: plant for purifying crude substance

Remote: inaccessible and sparsely populated

Seabed: ocean or sea floor

Solar cell: converts solar energy to electrical energy

Solar panel: device with connected solar cells

Steeply: in a sharp rise or fall manner

Subsistence: means of survival

Sustainable: capable of being maintained

Thermostat: regulates temperature automatically

Ultimately: as the end result

Unbleached: not artificially coloured or bleached

Viable: capable of being done with available means and circumstances

Windbreak: trees fence reducing wind force

Answers

Page 51 - True
Page 52 - Uranium
Page 53 - Hydroelectric power plant
Page 54 - True
Page 55 - True
Page 56 - True
Page 57 - False
Page 58 - False
Page 59 - False
Page 60 - Reduce, Reuse and Recycle
Page 61 - 1000
Page 62 - True
Page 63 - True
Page 64 - 1,706
Page 65 - Energy
Page 66 - False
Page 67 - Heating and cooling